Rejoicing In Hope

A Short History of the Life Of Hope Family Ministries

Contact Us:
hope@hopefamilyministries.com
(662)842-4673

Published by HFM
All Rights Reserved, 2019

Jo Ann Wilbanks, LPC

Dedication

Thank you, Father, for Mike, Rosemary, and Matt.
Thank you, Mike, Rosemary, and Matt for
your obedience to God.

Contents

Introduction

Hope

I love the name - what an incredible, wonderful concept. We're told over and over in the Bible that we have hope - always. We have hope in Christ. When trouble comes, we may need to be reminded, and we may need friends to come alongside us to remind us of that promise of hope. That's exactly what Hope Family Ministries is all about. There's a welcoming, family spirit here. Bro. Kevin walks over the parking lot praying for our clients to feel welcome when they get out of their cars and as they walk into the building. Our aim is to encourage and help, to point to Christ. When I first heard about Bro. Mike Marecle and Hope, I was so excited at the idea of a Christian Counseling Ministry! I admired Mike so much! His personal testimony is amazing. I thought - what a great idea! Through the years, I heard from people who'd been to see Mike or one of the other counselors and how *they'd been helped. I referred clients here, myself. Then, when I moved to Saltillo to be near my brand new granddaughter, I began to attend Calvary Baptist Church, where my son and his family go. I visited a ladies' Sunday School class where the teacher kept quoting Mike. I thought - she must be a client, but, no, she was Rosemary, his wife. She was a great teacher, and I enjoyed getting to know her so much. One day she told me Hope was needing to hire a part time counselor because Mike needed to retire. She said - you should apply! Working here is a dream come true for me! I can't believe I get to do it! What a privilege to serve the Lord by loving on His children! Bringing me here is just like Him, though! He is the best gift giver, planner, and coordinator ever! What a friend! What a Father! If you've ever thought about trusting Him with your life, I pray you'll do that.*

MAY THE GOD OF HOPE FILL YOU WITH
ALL JOY AND PEACE IN BELIEVING, SO
THAT YOU WILL ABOUND IN HOPE BY
THE POWER OF THE HOLY SPIRIT.

ROMANS 15:13

Mike Marecle
And
Hope Family Ministries

Mike Marecle is the founding president of Hope Family Ministries. God has used Mike in an amazing and mighty way to found a counseling ministry where there was none. At one time, Mike was a Harley riding, tool and die maker with a bad attitude and many prejudices. When he heard a preacher talk about God and his desire for a relationship with His children, Mike told him that he just wanted peace. He'd heard the preacher talk about the peace that God would give at salvation. That was something he'd never had. Mike explained to the preacher that he knew full well God would not want a relationship with him because he'd failed at every relationship in his life. He was convinced no one would want a relationship with him. Surprisingly though, of course, God did want a relationship. He pursued a relationship with Mike and kept pursuing a relationship until Mike learned to trust Him, his new Father. Then, He led him to seminary and used him to start a new ministry, Hope Family Ministries, in Tupelo, Mississippi.

Mike is a licensed, ordained, Southern Baptist minister. He is a board certified biblical counselor with the International Association of Biblical Counselors and a National Certified Christian counselor with the American Association of Christian Counselors. He holds a number of degrees from a number of schools, including a Doctorate of Ministry in Pastoral Counseling. Although, he says, "A lot of what I've learned has been on-the-job. Once I understand what God's calling me to do, I'll pursue that and see where I can get the skills I need." He says that his training in counseling has mainly come on-the- job, as with his tool and die making. He learned it on the job also. He worked in a machine shop for twenty three years. He said, "My first job was selling produce out of our garden and working on the farm during summers with my grandfather. When I turned sixteen, I worked at Thom McCann shoe store in the mall in Muscle Shoals, Alabama. I worked there till I finished high school." He worked because he didn't want to have to ask his parents for money; he wanted to be independent.

Mike says the night he graduated from high school, he drove all night to his dad's house in Michigan. He wanted to get to know his dad. He'd never had the chance to be around him. He stayed there and worked for a year at a couple of different jobs. His dad worked in a machine shop, so he was exposed to that trade. When he came back to North Alabama in 1973, jobs were scarce. The US economy was kind of in a holding pattern as everyone waited to see what would happen with the oil embargo. Mike's girlfriend's uncle knew a guy that owned a machine shop, and he told Mike to go there. He told him to tell the supervisor he had always wanted to be a tool and die maker. Mike didn't really know exactly what a tool and die maker did, but went ahead with the plan. He was hired as an apprentice for $1.65/hour and began working fifty-six hour weeks. Mike says he got fired after a couple of years at that job because he made a mistake. He misread a blueprint and drilled some holes in the wrong place in a piece of steel. Actually, the night shift supervisor and he didn't get along. He says, "Our philosophies didn't line up, but I was young, a jerk, and had a smart mouth. Getting fired did a lot to humble me. I was a better craftsman after that. I was more careful to do a better job because I knew I could get fired. Wherever I worked after that, I tried to be the best craftsman I could be on that job. I did that as long as I worked in that skilled trade."

Divorce

Mike married a girl whose father worked at Reynold's Metals, and he helped Mike get a job there. It was a good union job with good benefits. He worked there for three years. The marriage only lasted two years. He said the divorce hit him hard, "I guess I hit my threshold of rejection and failure. I decided I would never let anyone get close enough to hurt to me again." He bought a Harley Davidson motorcycle and began running with a rough crowd - drinking and getting high every day. He said, "I didn't set out to become an alcoholic or drug user. Along with treating the pain of the divorce, I was treating all the pain in my life, especially the pain from my childhood. From an early age, I didn't feel accepted in my mother's home or my daddy's home. They were both influenced by people they were married to at the time. I lived a rough lifestyle for several years. "

Remarriage

In 1979, Mike's sister, the only family member he was still in touch with, was working at the hospital in Russellville, Alabama. She told him she had met a fine Christian lady, Rosemary, from Booneville, Mississippi, and she wanted them to meet. He got her number and called her mainly because he knew how persistent his sister could be. "I'll come down there", he told Rosemary. "If you'll just open the door and let me make eye contact with you for a second, that'll get my sister off my back. You can leave the chain on the door!"

He said, "I wasn't sure about love at first sight, but something about being around her and her son Matt, who was three years old, made me want to be less destructive to myself. I knew I could trust her, and, at that time, I didn't trust anybody.

The facts that she was beautiful and we had chemistry were just icing on the cake!"

Mike said about his marriage to Rosemary, "We both came into marriage with unfinished business and a lot of emotional wounds. Somehow I knew I shouldn't let her get away though. We got married at the justice of the peace in Tuscumbia, Alabama. Little Matt went with us. In the back of my mind, I knew she'd leave me one day. Part of me wanted to let my guard down in that relationship, but part of me was really afraid to do that. Our relationship was kind of like a rollercoaster.

The first unconditional love I ever experienced was through Matt. He didn't care where I'd been, what I'd done. He loved me. God used him to peel some of the layers of mistrust and hurt I had built up off of me, so that I could learn how to love and be loved. I got laid off from Reynolds, had a great severance package, and didn't work for seven months. During that time, Matt and I just hung out."

Eventually, Mike went back to work in the tool and die trade in North Alabama. A few years later he went to work at General Electric in Columbia, Tennessee. A good friend had gone to work there. He kept telling Mike he needed to move there and work at GE with him because it was such a good place to work. Mike checked it out and found that it was a good place to work, with good benefits. He moved his family to Columbia, Tennessee.

Too Much Work

Mike was cautioned severely about working so much and encouraged to get his priorities in order. He did not appreciate the information. Before working at GE, he and a friend had opened a machine shop to do odd jobs part time. He worked and supervised in a shop fifty-six hours each week and then worked as many hours as physically possible in his own shop. After doing that for a while, his body rebelled. He was 30 years old. He saw a doctor because he thought he was having a stroke. His blood pressure was elevated, and the doctor was concerned about his health. He tried to give him wise counsel, but didn't mince words. The doctor told him that he didn't know what was going on in his life, but that if he didn't make peace with God, there was no need in putting money in any retirement program because he wasn't going to live long enough to need it. Mike said that just made him madder than he already was, but, in the days to come, the old man's words kept running through his mind.

Another Divorce?

When they'd been in Columbia about a year, Rosemary told Mike that she'd had enough and that he needed to leave. She couldn't handle his bad attitude and anger any more. She didn't want her son to grow up around a guy like him. He wasn't surprised. He knew in the back of his mind that this would happen someday. He went to church with them the next Sunday really just to buy himself some time until he could find a place to move to. He knew he couldn't change her mind. She had finished another degree by then, a bachelor's in nursing. She was a strong, independent womamn, and he knew she didn't need him.

Salvation

At church, he heard the preacher talk about peace. For the first time he considered there might be the potential for peace in his life. The preacher said that Jesus understands. "He knows where you've been and all you've done. He loves you and wants a relationship with you. If you'll let Jesus have His rightful place in your life, He'll give you peace." Mike says that it really didn't make sense to him, but he knew he wanted to hear more. He was drawn to the man and his message while simultaneously intimidated by the preacher's education, his intelligence, and his place of honor in the church. Mike said, "I watched him like I was an FBI agent looking for clues on a case! The more I watched him, the more I thought, 'Hey, this guy's for real! He's not just blowing smoke!' They had an invitation at the end of the service, but I didn't know about invitations. I had attended a Methodist church growing up. We didn't have invitations at the end of our services. I wasn't afraid to go down there where the preacher was, but I just didn't know how things worked. As I stood during the invitation, God caused me to realize my problem wasn't with money, my job, my mother, my dad, step-dad, my alcohol or drug problem, Matt's dad, Rosemary, or my history. My problem was I didn't have peace in my life. I needed peace. I just stood there. Very much under conviction."

That afternoon Mike told Rosemary that he didn't know what was going on, but he knew he had to talk to that preacher. He called the church and made an appointment for the following Thursday, April 17, 1987. Rosemary went with him to the church. He thought she went to make sure he didn't talk bad about her. He said, "I was not going to talk about our marriage. I needed to know if peace was available to me. I wanted to talk about how to find peace. I told the preacher, 'I'll do anything I need to do to find peace. I don't care what it takes. I need to tell you – I have failed in every relationship, some more than once. I just don't know or believe God wants a relationship with me. I'm not saying His death on the cross wasn't enough. It makes no sense to me that God would want a relationship or have any interest in me.'" The preacher shared Romans 5:8, "But God demonstrates His own love for us, in that while we were yet sinners, Christ died for us." He said, "'Mike, either God loves you and wants a relationship with you, or he's a liar.' I said, 'I don't know God; but, I know God's not a liar.'" The preacher also shared Jeremiah 10:23, "I know, O Lord that a man's way is not in himself, nor is it in a man who walks to direct his steps". The preacher explained that God makes the Holy Spirit available to us, so that we don't have to figure everything out or try to do life on our own.

Mike says, "I don't know what that guy prayed that day, but it all suddenly made so much sense, the way he explained everything. I asked God to forgive me. I said, 'God, you've been running the world all these years with no help from me. I know you don't need me, but I'm so tired from running my life. It may look good on the outside, but it's a mess on the inside. I'm tired of being angry, too. If you'll have my life, I'll give it to you!'" Mike says he saw stars like somebody had hit him in the head with a baseball bat. He didn't know what had happened, but there was no doubt something had. He says they finished up, thanked the preacher, and told him they'd see him Sunday. When he and Rosemary got outside, the release from all the stress and pressure he'd been under, thinking he had to figure everything out, hit him full force. He just started weeping. He said he had a lifetime of tears stored up, and the dam finally burst. Rosemary, who had never seen him cry except when his granddaddy died, was concerned. She said, "What's the matter with you?" He told her he didn't know, but that it was a good thing and that he'd be okay. He also said that he couldn't drive right then. She told him if he couldn't drive to let her drive. She'd take him to the ER!

What's Different?

When he went into work that afternoon, his boss, Billy, said, "How come you're not raising Hell like you always are? What's wrong with you?" Mike says he always wore his Harley shirt, a wallet with a chain, and a knife on his belt. He told his boss that nothing was wrong. He also told him that things were right for the first time in his life. He told him that he had met Jesus and had been saved. His boss was shocked and didn't believe him. Mike says that he was more shocked at himself for sharing that news. It felt good to him, though, and he thought he'd share again with his co-worker. He told his friend, Jerry, that he wanted to tell him about Jesus. Embarrassed, Jerry looked at the floor and admitted to Mike that he already knew Jesus. Mike chewed Jerry out for working right beside him and not trying to prevent him from going to Hell. When Jerry explained that he didn't know how to tell someone about Jesus, Mike assured him that he was going to learn how, and he would definitely train him.

Mike says, "I experienced a euphoric feeling that day, a buzz, unlike anything I'd ever experienced with drugs or alcohol. I thought, 'I can't believe this, talking about Jesus gives me such a rush! I've been looking for this in so many places! It can't be this simple!' My journey of witnessing began that day at GE. It was really neat to see how God revealed what he'd done in my life to the people around me at work. A black guy worked there that I had refused to help. I didn't think he knew his job, and I had given my boss a lot of grief for hiring him. After I came to know the Lord, I realized that prejudices I'd held all my life were not the way Jesus did business. I asked that guy to forgive me, and I helped him become a good tool and die maker. I led six to eight people to the Lord during the next two years that we lived there."

I'll Do Whatever You Want, God

Mike's story certainly doesn't end there. God was just getting started! Only a couple of months after he was saved, he told his pastor that he wasn't sure what was going on, but he'd had an experience he needed to talk to him about. He'd been inspired while reading in Matthew about where Peter was restored by Jesus after His resurrection. Peter had denied he knew the Lord three times in rapid succession before the crucifixion. After the resurrection, Jesus appeared to Peter, caused him to catch a bunch of fish, and grilled some up for their breakfast. It's in John 21. Around two o'clock, after work one morning, Mike was reading this passage in his Bible and felt the Lord's presence so intensely he thought he needed to just lie on the floor on his face. He felt the Lord ask him, "Mike, do you love me more than these?" Mike thought he meant people, things, anything else in the world. Mike said, "I'm willing to let you change whatever". He felt God said, "Mike, if I'm going to do what I want to do with you, you have to give up everything." He wanted to think about that a while and try to be sure before he jumped into something, but he sensed the door of opportunity closing. He told the Lord that, yes, he would surrender. He said, "I'll go where you want me to go and do whatever you want me to do." Mike says the preacher, sort of, believed him when he told about the experience. The preacher assured Mike that if God were calling him to full time ministry, He'd call Rosemary too. He assured him that he wouldn't divide his marriage. He told him to go to the minister of education at the church for discipling while waiting on God.

Mike: I understand you're the minister of education.

Minister: Yep, that's right.

Mike: I need you to teach me how to walk by faith.

Minister: Read your Bible and pray.

Mike: That's cheap, man! If that's all you know, maybe we need to get somebody else to teach people around here!

Minister: No. Wait. Here is a book. Take it and read it, but be sure to bring it back.

Mike: Man, I'll give you a deposit for the book!

Three days later, Mike had read the book and returned it. Next, he read through the minister of education's personal library. Then, he read through the church library. He couldn't get enough training and bible study!

When his church began EE, Evangelism Explosion, a witnessing training program, only four months after his salvation, Mike was in his element. All the church staff were involved. The class met for training and then went out in small groups to homes to witness. Mike says he had to learn to be sensitive to the Spirit. He was very aggressive as a witness at first. He loved witnessing and training people to witness. He felt he had found his place, his niche in God's kingdom.

We Know We've Been Called

He couldn't rest easily though because of the experience he'd had that he believed was a call to vocational ministry sixteen months earlier. He decided not to speak to Rosemary about it. He felt that it needed to be something God led her to. He says, "I knew if she was going to walk out of her dream home we'd built, it'd be God, not me, that got her to do that. I asked God to have her write me a note. That way I could go back and read it over and over". Mike said, "One day I opened my Bible to a note from her". She had quoted Oswald Chambers. 'Most of us walk around in a fog even though we know we've been called'. He had his answer from Rosemary and from God. As they were walking a few days later, Rosemary said, "When will we put the house up for sale?" Mike said, "Why would we do that?" Rosemary said, "If we're going to do what God wants us to, we're going to have to go to seminary."

Oswald Chambers in My Utmost for His Highest wrote,
"When God speaks, many of us are like men in a fog, we give no answer...
Be ready for the sudden surprise visits of God.
A ready person never needs to get ready.
Think of the time we waste trying to get ready when God has called!"

*I couldn't have said
it better.*

*I Love you
Rosemary*

1/3/89

Seminary

Mike wondered what seminary would take a journeyman tool and die maker with only a high school education. Plus, he and Rosemary both had been divorced.

Most church members didn't believe God would call people, who were in their second marriage, to vocational ministry. Southwestern Baptist Theological Seminary in Fort Worth, Texas, had a program for people who are called later in life. Mike could work toward an Associate of Divinity Degree, but he'd be in classes with master's level students. He wouldn't have different classes, he'd just receive a different degree. With questions looming in their minds, they asked God to make it crystal clear to them whether they were to make the move and attend the seminary.

Rosemary set up a job interview at Saint Joseph Hospital in Fort Worth. They also made an appointment for Mike to interview with a representative of Southwestern. She was hired on the spot at her interview. They agreed to hold her job for a few months until she and Mike could move there, and they agreed to give her a one thousand dollar sign-on bonus. Mike told the representative at Southwestern that he had no doubt about God's will in sending him there. He told him that he would gladly stand outside under the trees and listen to the teachers if he had to. The representative thought for a few minutes and told Mike that he had the power to accept him. His signature was all that was required, and he was going to give it!

Rosemary told Mike that they needed to get the house ready to sell. Mike told her that God knew their need for a buyer, and he wanted to just put a sign in the yard. Ten days after placing a sign in their yard, they received a call from a realtor who said that she had a client, moving from out of town. She said that she had shown her several houses, but none were satisfactory. She asked if she could show theirs. Mike told her she would not receive a commission, but she wanted to show it anyway. The buyer's father, who was a builder, came with her to see the house. He pointed out many good things about the house and encouraged her to buy it. She bought it for the asking price and agreed to let them continue to live in it until their planned move.

The money for seminary came from an odd situation with that same house. Two years earlier, about the time Mike was saved, they put a contract on a house that was being built. The builder was from Texas. He was in the area building some houses and was building this one for himself. It was unfinished, so Rosemary got to choose light fixtures and colors. It was almost finished when the builder agreed to let them go ahead and move in a couple of weeks before closing. The realtor called one day and said, "We've got a problem." Mike said, "Who is we?" "Your builder has left town and is not coming back. I think you need to talk to a lawyer. I think he has breached his contract." "Okay, what about us living in the house?" "I don't know."

Mike talked to a lawyer and discovered that the house was in limbo, really. Within the next few months, it was repossessed from the builder by his mortgage company while they were living in it rent free. Finally, Mike realized he'd have to go to the court house steps and buy it at auction, which he'd never done before. He didn't know the details of that. He discussed it with a lawyer who advised against it. Cash is required to purchase at auction, and Mike would need to get a mortgage. Mike prayed about it and thought about it. He planned to go ahead and try to buy it at the auction. He planned to trust God with the details of the sale. On the day of the auction, he went to the courthouse steps and raised the price just a few dollars to make his bid. No one else bid, so he won the house. He didn't really know what to do next, but a man from his mortgage company was there also. He told Mike to write a personal check for the house, and he could go ahead and complete his application for a loan with his company. They had begun the process, but had put it on hold while the details of the house had been worked out. They paid twelve or thirteen thousand less than they had originally agreed to. That was the money God used to help them go through seminary.

Another New House

During the two years in Texas, God broke Mike and humbled him many times.

He would get up in the mornings, and say to God, "I don't have a clue what's going on, but I'm going to trust you today." God never failed in his provision for him and his family. Rosemary had asked that they not live in an apartment or student housing. When they moved to Texas, they pulled up to a realtor's office with a U-Haul truck full of their stuff. The realtor took them around to some houses to see if they could find one they liked. They did like a house they saw two blocks from the school they wanted Matt to attend. The house was brand new and had never sold even though it had been on the market for two years. Mike spoke with the owner and asked if he could let the realtor hold money for the closing, rent the house until closing, and move in that day. By that afternoon, they had the keys to a brand new house and started moving in.

Mike had also prayed for a friend for Rosemary since she'd be so far from family and friends during this time. As they were unloading their U-Haul, a lady who lived down the street pulled up. She was from Columbus, Mississippi, about ninety minutes from Rosemary's hometown. She and Rosemary became friends instantly and made many trips home during the two years they lived in Texas. She invited them to her church where they soon joined. Their seminary years tested their marriage, but was good for it because it forced them to depend on each other.

Mike successfully completed his degree, but still had no idea where he would serve. He didn't have peace about being a pastor of a church, because of his earlier divorce. He didn't want to potentially divide a church. He pursued evangelism, but never felt that preaching was God's will for him. They moved to Tupelo, Mississippi, where Rosemary went to work in home health, and he went to work in a local factory in tool and die. He felt at times that he should give back his degree and license, along with his ordination papers because nothing seemed to be happening. He was teaching Sunday school, working in discipleship training, yet God was not using him in vocational ministry. He felt God was saying, "Why won't you let walking with me day to day be enough for you? Why won't you let what I say about you be enough?" He would tell God, "I don't know; help me do that". Mike feels that the first eight years of his being a Christian were years of God's bringing items from his buried past to the surface and helping him deal with them. God was teaching him to forgive those who'd wronged him, and to ask forgiveness of those he had wronged. All along, he was increasing skills for processing life through faith and scripture.

In 1994, Mike went with some friends to the Promise Keepers' march on the Mall in Washington, D.C., which was a significant experience for him. A few months later he and Rosemary went on a couples' marriage retreat. Then they attended an Experiencing God event where they heard Henry Blackaby speak in Memphis. After these, Mike and Rosemary were led to rededicate their marriage to the Lord. Then in 1995, he attended a Walk to Emmaus spiritual retreat where participants spend three days in fellowship, prayer and Bible study with no phones or watches. The focus is on Christian love, having your spiritual eyes open to God's presence and His work around you. Mike said, "On the second day they have an event called 'dying moments' where they invite you to offer a piece of bread as a symbol of something you need or want to give to the Lord." Mike struggled with understanding what the

Lord wanted him to give up, but he knew there was something. He was very emotional. He went outside with a guy. The man wanted to help and kept asking him what was wrong. Mike just kept saying he didn't know.

Mike: I don't know. I don't know. I don't know.

God: Mike, I just want you to surrender. Be content with living right now. Don't worry about tomorrow.

Mike: I will surrender.

He went home and told Rosemary that he didn't think he'd be working as a tool and die maker much longer.

Rosemary: What do you mean?

Mike: I don't know. I don't know. I don't know.

A Counseling Ministry

Around this time Mike's neighbor told him that he needed to be available to help people. He said, "You counsel people all the time". Mike had never thought of himself as a counselor. He tried to help people. He identified with them and loved them. He wanted to help them find hope and direction. He would use scripture and prayer to try to guide and encourage people. His neighbor's words kept coming back to him. He went to his pastor and Sunday school teacher to tell them about his idea for starting a faith based, biblical counseling ministry. His pastor suggested he talk to an attorney who was also a deacon in their church, Greg Pirkle.

Mike made an appointment to see Mr. Pirkle. He was very impressed because the office was located on the seventh floor of the bank building downtown, and he was served coffee in a china cup. Mr. Pirkle was gracious and told Mike that his own dad was a pastor. He also told Mike that he reminded him of evangelists who used to visit their home. He said, "I think what you're talking about doing has been needed in this area for a long time. If you want to be available to help people, we can set up a nonprofit. People can make donations. You'll need six people to serve on the board. You'll need to come up with a name for the ministry." During the next few weeks, the word "Hope" kept coming up in different ways to Mike. On one occasion, Rosemary told him that people came to see him without hope and when they left, they had hope. She thought he should name the ministry, "Hope". Mike thought, "We're all about reconciliation, families, and ministry, so the name 'Hope

Family Ministries' seems right". Mr. Pirkle had warned him that it was typical to get turned down the first time when applying for nonprofit status. He filed, and the request went through the first time. Hope Family Ministries became a nonprofit, May 12, 1995. The following is a list of those who have served on the board: Dottie Carnathan, Kim Chrestman, Linda Hale, Dr. Eric Harding, Carol Harding, Anne Harrington, James Hayes, Ellen Johnston, Merrill Johnston, Dr. Bill Kalhstorf, Joy Kellum, Dr. Martin Lee, Missy Lunceford, Rosemary Marecle, James Ed Mattox, Dr. Mary Carol Miller, Jim Nolting, Carol Nolting, Al Pleasants, Mark Smith, Dr. Linda Southward, Lisa Tally, Robert Upchurch, Joann Upchurch, Dr. Charles Wikle, and Dr. Ronnie Young.

Mike worked fifty hours each week at his machine shop job and counseled Saturdays and Sunday afternoons, out of their home, whenever he could schedule clients. He did that for three or four months. He had more work than he could possibly get done. He had an accident at work and was off work four weeks, during which time he prayed for direction. After returning to work after the accident, his boss insisted he work four - ten hour days. He counseled on Mondays at his home and worked forty hours each week at the shop after that.

When it came time to renew his homeowners insurance, he could not renew because of the liability issue involved in running a counseling ministry out of his home. Mike decided it was time to move out. He rented an office in Tupelo for $250/month. He says,

"We didn't have that much money. I told God that I would need help. A supporter brought a check for $500, so I had enough money. A former client furnished the office. We moved after a year to a bigger office. By that point I was working full time in the ministry. We hired a part time secretary. We were down there about two years, before it became obvious that we needed another counselor. We hired a retired pastor."

I Do Not Want to Build a Building

Mike said, "The office was in such a noisy, downtown area, right on a corner. We could hear people walking by, talking. We could hear all the trains. We began to pray and ask God if we should buy a building, rent a bigger office, or build a building. I put that last in there because I wanted to have three options. I did not want to build! The board and I entered into a sixty day season of prayer about the project."

Five weeks into the season of prayer, a deacon in the church called to ask if Mike could fill in as a speaker at a Lion's Club luncheon. He didn't want to take time out to do that! He was very busy, and had a lot of counseling scheduled for that week. He felt he should go, though. He spoke for ten minutes on his testimony and ten minutes on the ministry. He was aggravated because the guy who introduced him mispronounced his name and then told them he was a Methodist. He didn't feel he'd done a great job, but went on his way. That afternoon the guy who had asked him to speak called. He said, 'Mike that was the most powerful testimonies I've ever heard. A guy in our club wants to give you land for your ministry.'

Mike: 'Really, what's his name?'

'James Mattox.'

'Where's the land?'

'Probably down on Mattox Street.'

Mike called Mr. Mattox.

Mr. Mattox: "That's one of the most powerful testimonies I've ever heard. When you were talking, God told me to give you land for your ministry."

Mike: (thinking this won't work and I don't want to build a building) "I'll have to take this to our board of directors and we'll pray about it."

Mr. Mattox: "Great."

They met the following morning. Mike says he got into Mr. Mattox's Suburban. As they began to talk, he began to feel as if he'd known him all his life. Mike asked him how much land he planned to give. Mr. Mattox told him that he would give him as much as he would need now and what he might need in the future. He showed Mike three different sites. He explained where he thought would be the best site for a building. Mike was thinking to himself that he didn't want to build a building and that he didn't have time to build a building!

Mike presented the news about the potential gift to the board, and God impressed upon him that this land was where he wanted the ministry. In August, 1999 they transferred the deed. Mr. Mattox and he walked outside after the deal was finished. Mr. Mattox told him, "I know my parents in heaven are rejoicing to know that part of our old family farm is being used in the ministry."

Mike had been advised that once the ministry owned the $50,000 piece of property, he had board approval for the floor plan, and they raised an additional $50,000, they could secure a loan to build a building. He didn't want the board to have to sign for the loan. He wanted the bank to accept his signature alone. He checked in with God a time or two about signing his name on the $250,000.00 contract. They broke ground on the building on Mike's forty-fifth birthday, October 8, 1999.

Mike is assured that God worked ahead of him in many ways and prepared the way for the ministry. Mike and the board consulted with several counselors in the area who willingly gave their indispensable opinions about the lay out and flow of the building to optimize clients' comfort and anonymity.

J.B. Etheridge, owner of Corinthian Furniture, was in Mike's Sunday school class.

J.B: "Preacher, my daddy taught me if a man helps you, you ought to help him."

Mike: "Yes, sir. I believe that too."

J.B: "I've grown more since you've been teaching our class the last few years than I have in thirty years of Sunday school. I'm going to give you the furniture you need for your building."

They visited his son, Vick, at Corinthian Furniture. He told his son, "We're going to give him whatever he wants". Another businessman, Larry Stewart, whose advice was invaluable all the way through the project, made an interior decorator available for the building.

A former client, who was an artist, donated several framed pieces of art for the building.

Mike says, "I felt I needed to do something. I'd gone to Corinth and picked out furniture. I said that I would go pick it up, but they said, 'No, we deliver'! When we moved into the building, they delivered twenty-four pieces of furniture. In July of 2000 we moved into the new building." It was not always easy, though. "There were times that God turned the cookie jar upside down and poured it out, so to speak. There were times He seemed to hide the jar, and I couldn't find it anywhere. A 4,400 square foot facility took time and money to keep up. It was a struggle to counsel, raise support, manage the business and meet with the board." His supporters encouraged him to let people know what God was doing. "He will provide," they said. Mike created a newsletter. Each month he'd type the newsletter himself. Then he'd go to the church to run off copies, fold them, address them, and stamp and mail them. Mike would not wish on anyone what God asked of him during that season, but would not take anything for what God did during that time. "I've had several times of desperation, questioning myself, and thinking, 'Do I need to step out of the way?' God's been faithful to guide and to provide."

Mike's Early Life

Mike's mother grew up in an alcoholic home. His grandparents were good people; they came from good families. Unfortunately, alcohol had an impact. He thinks that's where he got his 'party genes'. His mother quit school when she was fourteen and married his dad who was seventeen. They lived on his grandparents' farm. His dad went into the Marine Corps soon after the marriage. Living on the farm was an awesome experience for a little boy. He had his own horse! He and his grandfather rode horses. Five or six other families lived on and worked for the farm. His grandfather was his hero. He wanted to be like him, so he would steal beer and cigarettes. He knows he started using alcohol and smoking cigarettes before he was five because he remembers doing that before starting first grade. He began first grade at the age of five. He liked the way alcohol made him feel; it calmed him down. He thinks he probably had ADHD, along with a lot of other stuff.

As a child Mike reached out to the adults in his life for comfort or protection, but they were either not available or had their own stuff going on. He began to look for ways to comfort himself, to feel less chaotic. Using alcohol was one of those ways. His grandmother and mother seemed to always be on his case about something. His granddad was always coming to his rescue. He believes he had a real problem with female authority figures because of this. He avoided them and certainly didn't look to them for comfort or acceptance. He was very mischievous, a dare devil. He thinks he probably didn't think before acting until his late twenties.

He was introduced to sexuality at a very young age, probably age five or six, by a boy who lived on the farm. He says that some people shut down that part of themselves when they're introduced to sexuality at a young age. For others, it becomes a source of comfort or self-medication, and it was for him. He says that 'feeding that monster' became a way of life for him before he knew anything about all that stuff.

You Should Know

He feels his mom must have thought he was supposed to be preprogramed when he showed up. Many times she would tell him, "You should know that." The problem was, he didn't know already. He felt tricked and his frustration and injustice turned to anger. He had a happy-go- lucky side and a dark side that was all about self-medication and numbness. Shame became an integral part of his life. Through self-condemnation, shame would lead him to numbness, which, to him, was better than emotional pain. Self-condemnation became another tool to keep from feeling disconnected. Mike feels he was like "the double minded man" mentioned in James, chapter one. He was "unstable in all his ways".

Mike says that his mom wasn't around a lot during his early childhood. She went back to high school and then finished nursing school. In those days, women were required to live on campus. He lived on the farm with his grandparents and two sisters. He saw his dad only a couple of times during that five year period. He learned to live without his dad in his life. After his parents divorced, his dad remarried and had four more children. They lived in Chicago, then Michigan. He didn't remember anyone telling him not to speak of him, but somehow he knew it was not allowed. He didn't understand what had gone wrong in the marriage. He wondered whether he'd done something wrong to cause his dad to leave. He loved his mother and grandparents and couldn't hold any of them responsible for anything bad. As a small child, he didn't know how to blame someone for something bad and love them simultaneously. He ended up blaming himself.

Mike remembers that it was only after his mother finished the nursing program at Northeast that she told her children she'd been secretly married for a year already. She couldn't be in the nursing program if she were married. On his eighth birthday the family moved from his grandparents' farm to Tuscumbia, Alabama, which was a big adventure for him. His stepfather had family there and drove a truck for a company that was located there. Mike says that he and his stepdad got along fine while he was away from the house, driving a truck. After the marriage, his relationship with his mother was more complicated. He felt she did love him, but he felt pushed back when his stepdad was home. She was a different person when he was there. Mike says the drawing closer and then being pushed away continued until five years before her death, when she finally forgave his biological father.

Mike says his stepdad had some good qualities. He was a good man and provided for his family; however, he was emotionally frozen. Mike and the other children had to be careful around him to try to keep from setting him off about something. He was not affectionate. He touched Mike only when he was showing him how to do something or disciplining him. He told him he loved him only a couple of times. During one of those times his stepdad was dying of cancer and was possibly confused. Mike did appreciate some aspects of their relationship. He respects his stepdad for making him work, not allowing him to divide him and his mother and for holding him responsible for his choices.

At some point in their relationship, Mike realized he was not going to be able to be the guy his stepdad wanted him to be, so he decided to be the opposite. He remembers thinking that he didn't want to be a problem or enjoy being a problem, but he always felt he was a problem. As a teenager, he would buy whiskey from the local bootlegger and go camping, where he would drink all weekend. Many nights he and his friends would just drive around and drink. He became a pathological liar. He lied so often that he believed his own lies. He was using pornography and felt an incredible rage on the inside. He says that run-ins with the police were not unusual for him. He remembers coming home from the first grade to a police car in the driveway. Some damage had been done to a playground at the Catholic School and everyone assumed he had done it. He says that time he was innocent. His stepdad was very controlling. They had a battle of the wills. He was determined that if Mike lived in his house, things were going to be his way. There wasn't physical abuse, but he feels there was emotional abuse. His step dad had a look that said - you should be ashamed of yourself. During his adolescent period, he would call his dad in Chicago whose life Mike describes as 'relationally, just one train wreck after another'. Mike's dad would put his mother and step-dad down when he talked about them to kind of pick Mike up. That was just like pouring gas on the fire of his discontent.

I'll Stay Till I Graduate

Mike remembers one particular argument over sideburns during which his stepdad drew a line on each side of his face with a permanent marker indicating exactly where his sideburns should come to. Somehow Mike ended up on the floor with his stepdad sitting on top of him. Mike hated his stepdad, and says he would have killed him if he could have gotten away with it. His mother put him and his sister, Laura, in the car and they rode around until he could promise her he would stay at home till he finished high school. He hated being at home and began working as much as possible to avoid being there. He started working in a shoe store at the age of sixteen. He would work till nine o'clock at night. He did not want to have to ask his parents for money. He wanted to buy his own clothes and other essentials.

He did keep his promise to his mother. He stayed at home until graduation. The night he graduated, he drove all night to his dad's house in Michigan in a car he had bought for seventy-five dollars. He remembers driving over a hill by his house, feeling as if he were out of jail, and promising to never spend the night in that house again.

Mike understands now that he was dealing with the overflow of unfinished business in the lives of both his parents and his stepparents. He asked forgiveness of his mother and stepdad after his salvation. He wanted their relationships to be healed, but he still did not enjoy being around them. He was troubled about it so much that he spoke with a counselor about it. The counselor asked him if he dishonored his parents in the way he lived his life. Mike told him that he had done that in the past, but not in the present time. The counselor said that maybe that's all God expects. He doesn't expect you to fix those relationships. Mike says a huge burden of guilt and shame was lifted off him that day as he heard those reassuring words.

Robbie

At age eleven or twelve, his sister, Robbie, who was just fifteen months older than Mike, became very sick. She was diagnosed with Ewing Sarcoma, which is a rare cancer that occurs most frequently in teenagers and young adults. She was in and out of a Memphis hospital for about a year and half before she died, just three days before her fourteenth birthday. She was buried on her birthday. He and his sister lived with Maw and Pop, their grandparents, and other relatives while their mother stayed in Memphis with Robbie. Mike says that, until she died, he didn't know she had cancer or that she might possibly die. He assumed she would come home after her stay in the hospital. He remembers that one day his mother and stepdad showed up at the farm with all Robbie's things. He asked where she was. They told him that she wasn't coming home because she was in Heaven. After the funeral, their rooms were switched. His room was moved to where his sisters had slept, and his younger sister was now sleeping in what was previously his room. His mother went back to work and life continued. There was no discussion about her death. He doesn't remember pictures of her in the house.

Mike remembers his real dad, along with his new wife and children, came to the funeral, but his presence caused a stir. He had not visited Robbie, his daughter, in the hospital, so Mike's mom thought he didn't need to be there. Mike couldn't look at or visit with his father until the appropriate time. He inadvertently upset his stepfather because he jokingly asked a cousin, who had passed a suit down to him, if he remembered that particular suit. His stepfather fumed because he thought it was a slight against him and made him look like a bad provider.

After they moved to Tuscumbia, Mike's family had started going to a Methodist church. He attended confirmation classes and was confirmed. He says he went through with that because he didn't want to go to Hell. Also, he knew the wrath that awaited him at home if he didn't participate. He would be bringing shame and failure on the family, supposedly.

Music played a huge role in Mike's life during his teen years. He admits that he was too clumsy and nervous to do well in sports and usually got hurt when he tried to play basketball or football. His mother inherited his great grandfather's piano, and so he and his sisters took piano lessons. After he was hurt in football in ninth grade, his parents suggested he join the band. He played trombone his last three years of high school. He says that music is the language of emotion. He has always felt connected through it; he loves it.

Mike says, "The good news is that God has not wasted anything that has happened in my life. I've been in the kingdom thirty-one years. I needed and wanted a Father. There has not been one situation where I have been disappointed as I have looked to God to be my father. I experienced what a person is supposed to experience with a father, through learning about God and who He says I am. He tells us what He expects and gives us what we need to accomplish it. There is no condemnation. No threats. No shame. My past is never brought up. My sins are as far as the East is from the West, and they are remembered no more. God taught me how to live without anger, inappropriate sexuality, alcohol, or drugs controlling my life. God told me over and over, 'Mike, it's going to be okay; you don't have to be angry anymore.'"

A Journeyman Christian?

After working as an apprentice and then a journeyman in a skilled trade, I understood the journeyman process. I began to look around for a journeyman Christian. The minister of education, the youth minister, and the pastor at my church all became my mentors. I believed God was big enough to heal all. I had made bad choices, but I saw in scripture that He could use me however He wanted. The first eight years after I was saved were really my healing journey. I did bible studies on how to manage anger, be a godly man, pray, be a godly husband, and be a godly daddy. I didn't know how to do any of those; I had to learn. I became a different person. God broke me to the point where I would let walking with Him today be enough. I would let what He says about me be enough. He gives me faith and puts the Fruit of the Spirit in my life. Living that way was the goal. Every thirty minutes, I would check to see if I had the Fruit of the Spirit. If I did, I'd try to go another thirty minutes. If one were missing, I'd ask forgiveness. I'd tell God I trusted Him to finish the good work He'd started in my life. Having a clear conscience that I'd done what He told me or that I'd fixed it. God guarded my heart and mind with peace that passed understanding. He gave me wisdom. He told me in scripture that if I humbled myself, he'd raise me up. I pursued humility and tried to walk by faith. He gave me many opportunities to tell about Jesus. That desire came about when God saved me, and that's been my focus.

One thing I had to learn to do - I had to stop romanticizing memories of partying, pride and self-sufficiency. I asked God to take the desire to drink and smoke away. He did. God gave me the tools I needed to not need alcohol, but it was my job to put those tools into practice. I struggled with pornography, too. Remembering that women are created in the likeness of God and that sex outside marriage doesn't have the payoff Satan says it does, has helped me overcome that battle. The battlefield is in the mind though. I have to take every thought captive. Philippians 4:8 says, "Finally, brethren, whatever is true, whatever is honorable, whatever is right, whatever is pure, whatever is lovely, whatever is of good repute, if there is any excellence and if anything worthy of praise, dwell on these things". If I have scripture in my thoughts, Satan doesn't have room to put impure thoughts. I meditate on the law and talk about scripture; God's Spirit takes care of the rest.

I came to a point where I had to accept the person God made me to be. I had to decide that I was okay with how he made me. I had to learn to love myself and not hate myself. In the eyes of everyone around me, something was wrong with me. I had so much guilt and shame that I hated myself. Coming to rest in my soul about me was a big step. Jesus didn't forgive my sins and save me so that everything would be about me. There is a normal process that results in my resting in my soul about myself. In Matthew 11:28, Jesus says, "Come to Me, all who are weary and heavy laden, and I will give you rest". It took a lot of work and time, but His rest became such a sweet spot in my walk with the Lord."

Rosemary

With Two of the Original Board Members

Merrill and Ellen Johnston

Rosemary

Before all this came to fruition, we lived in Muscle Shoals, Alabama. Mike had told me he was saved before we married, but then he wouldn't go to church with me. He had this job offer in Columbia, Tennessee. I told him I'd move there with him if he'd go to church with me. We moved and we both had good jobs. I was over the ER there. We started going to church at First Baptist, and we loved it. Not long after that he said he wanted to go see the preacher. We both went and he prayed the salvation prayer. Since he worked the evening shift, they asked him to help with Bible School. He worked with some strong Christian ladies. The guy that was over education began to disciple Mike. I knew God was working in his life. It wasn't long before he began feeling called into the ministry. I wrote him a note and stuck it in his Bible, telling him I supported him in whatever God was calling him to. That's when events leading up to the ministry seemed to fall into place. It wasn't long after the note, we tacked a 'For Sale' sign on our mailbox. Within a few days, a realtor sold our house to a lady from out of town. The money from that house paid for Mike's seminary.

I interviewed with a Catholic hospital near the seminary. They agreed to hold a place for me on day shift. In those days a day shift job was rare. When our house sold a month early, I called the lady I'd interviewed with, and she told me to come on to work. We pulled up to a realty company in a nearby town known for its good schools. Matt was in about seventh grade. The realtor called a builder she knew who had been sitting on a few houses he'd been unable to sell. She thought he might rent one to us until we could close on it. We moved into another brand new house that very day. It was smaller than the one we'd had, but it was all we needed. Mike started to work there also. He found a job near the seminary and worked the afternoon shift that fit in with his school.

Friends at seminary thought Mike was going to be an evangelist, but we didn't think so. I talked to one church myself, Mike wasn't home, about an assistant pastorate in South Carolina. We prayed about it, but ended up not taking that. I said let's just go home and see what God leads us to. We bought a house in Tupelo that needed some work. I got a job at the hospital in Tupelo, and he began working in tool and die again. People began coming to our house for counseling every night of the week. I'd be in the kitchen cooking supper and he'd be counseling in the living room. I'd say, "Y'all want to eat supper with us?" Our neighbor and his two adopted sons had been coming to Mike for counseling, and he gave Mike a $500 check. That was kind of the start of the ministry.

Then, while he was in his first little office downtown, someone left $10,000 cash in an envelope behind the plant in the waiting room. That was the first big donation. All during our marriage, we tried to live on one salary. I always thought we'd starve if Mike went full time with the counseling ministry. I'm sure that was just Satan giving me those doubts. I began working for Gilbert's Home Health around the time Mike began counseling so much. I enjoyed working there for seven years. Then, when it was time for Matt to go to college, we visited Mississippi College and a few others. He felt that's where the Lord was leading him. I said, "There's no way! It's too expensive!" He was able to get seventy-five percent of his fees paid by scholarships. God provided in ways we couldn't have imagined. Then we used savings bonds that I had been buying along through the years to finish out paying for his college.

We have generous donors who are people Mike has helped from way back. You know some people who come in have no way to pay. They're in such a bad place when they come in. There's not a lot of cash reserve, but Hope Ministries has always made its payroll. We're the only place in town that does donation based, Christian Counseling. A lot of pastors in the area will counsel someone a time or two, then send them to us.

Matt is gifted in and enjoys finding funding, and it looks like God's going to take care of that through him. He and his wife, Natalie, met at Mid America Seminary, where she was training to become a missionary. He got a business degree from MC and worked for a food service company for a year. It was clear that business wasn't his calling. After seminary, Matt pastored a church in Booneville for seven years. Then, he decided to work for the Home Mission Board, and they moved to Kansas City. They both took secular jobs to support themselves, but they only lived there two years before moving to Springdale, Arkansas. Natalie had a sister in Springdale. Matt worked in his brother-in-law's cabinet shop, and Natalie taught school. He did supply preaching part time, but he wasn't in full time ministry. When Mike needed help at Hope Ministries badly, we all prayed about Matt's moving his family back to Tupelo.

It ended up being the perfect thing for all of us. I inherited some money around that time, and we were able to help them buy a house right away. Around that time, Mike had open heart surgery, and we all realized he could not keep the pace he'd been keeping, working as many hours. He was going to need help. It ended up working out just fine. All along the way, I've been the one just watching it unfold. I feel like my role has been one of support. It is incredible how many people come up to me all the time, thank me, and tell me how they've been helped. We haven't starved after all either!

**Matt Wilburn at the Hope Awareness Kick Off Luncheon
(Matt explains future plans)**

Our ultimate goal for the future is to help our donors and supporters heal families through God's hope by placing biblical counseling tools into the hands of moms, dads, pastors, families, and congregations. Hope Family Ministries has provided counseling and produced some of the best biblical counseling resources to help with the deepest needs here in Tupelo for more than twenty-four years. We have a first-class facility and a great staff. Thousands of people have been served here on a donation basis. We want to make these time-tested tools available to churches, prisons, groups, classes, clubs, and organizations all over the world. We want to come alongside pastors, when needed, and work toward helping church members become healthy. We are in a fund-raising phase right now to build a new building to produce resources for people who don't live in our region. We want to offer our curriculum on multiple platforms. Finally, we want to make sure these services are available decades from now, leaving a legacy of healing.

Our Client Jena Pennington (along with her five, yes five, children)

One client, Jena Pennington, shared her story of healing at the kick-off luncheon.

Her story follows:

SGT Andrew Tyler Pennington served in the United States Marine Corps for nine years before leaving the service in 2012 to be with his family. He served in Iraq and deployed to numerous other locations. He died on April 3, 2015. He committed suicide, leaving a young wife, pregnant with twin boys, and three small children.

Jo Ann Wilbanks, LPC

I Can't Breathe

Today was the day
I can't think straight
Like a fog is rolling in
Is this really my fate?

Complete darkness surrounds me
Today was the day
I can't think straight
Like a fog is rolling in
Is this really my fate?

Complete darkness surrounds me
Deafening silence and still
Where is everyone
Is this really God's will?

I find myself in an ocean
Complete chaos and confusion
This fog has become a storm
A surreal optical illusion

The storm is getting bigger
Creating waves, growing stronger
They begin crashing against me
I can't fight much longer.

They're knocking me down
I can't swim, I'm trying
No one can see me
I'm fighting, but I'm dying

I can't breathe any more
My chest hurts from crying
My body is going numb

This is absolutely terrifying

I'm screaming for help
But no one can hear me
I'm exhausted from fighting
Can't this be over, set me free

One final wave
Would be the end of it all
I can't breathe, I'm drowning
I close my eyes and embrace the fall

Jena Pennington

I wrote that poem three and a half years ago, the same week I lost my husband, Tyler, to suicide. I discovered writing was an outlet for me, a way to express what I was feeling and what was going on in my mind. Instead of bottling it up, it helped to release it on paper. I didn't really have anyone to talk to, so writing was my escape. I would literally just sit and stare at a blank wall. I wasn't really processing what was going on around me. I prayed every day and begged God to take the pain away, to bring him back. I didn't think anyone could understand what I was going through. I had gotten online, hoping to find help, answers, or support, but I discovered there were no others like me. There was no one out there that fit my description. I was pregnant with twin boys at the time. We already had three children. I was alone, pregnant, and trying to survive my husband's suicide, all while trying to take care of three grieving children and my own grief. I literally had to take each day at a time, moment by moment. Every minute of every day I would go over in my head; breathe, eat, sleep, repeat. That's the only way I could survive those first few weeks. I was the twins' lifeline and they were mine. I knew that in order for them to survive, I had to survive. That's what I did. I felt so accomplished when I would make it through another day. We survived that entire pregnancy with very few complications. Granted, it wasn't peaches and cream, but with the help of my parents and my siblings, we made it. They were born perfect and healthy, "textbook twins" as the specialist called them. They were the biggest twins the NICU had ever seen, and they were mine. I did it!

With two newborns came new challenges, though, new emotions, new griefs. My daily list had to adjust with their schedule. There wasn't much time to write anymore, so more of my emotions and feelings got bottled up. I prayed and prayed for God to help me. With all the joy that comes with new babies, there was so much sadness over what we were missing, what Tyler was missing. I kept questioning over and over why God would give me these precious babies if he knew what we were going to go through. Along with the stress of newborns and juggling all these new emotions, I was exhausted. It almost seemed impossible to live like that anymore, so I got online again and searched for help. I researched grief and how to process it, and there it was, a grief process list: denial, anger, bargaining, depression, and acceptance. Awesome! Another list. I thought I could do that. I survive with lists. I'm a bit OCD. I thrive in order and routine. That's how I survived the beginning of the tragedy, so that's how I could continue to survive. I thought that if I could just hit each of the milestones of grief and check them off one by one, I'd be good! Little did I know, grief doesn't work that way. I discovered it's full of unpredictable twists and turns. They blindside you, like a rollercoaster headed to complete darkness. Just when I thought I was doing better and had moved on to the next step, I would lose my grip and fall again. I was so sad and so lost. I prayed so hard to understand why I couldn't complete the steps like everyone else. Why couldn't I have the fulfillment of crossing each level of grief off my list? It wasn't fair. I didn't know if I would survive it anymore. I didn't want to die, but I didn't want to live anymore either. My children were suffering; I was suffering. It was all too much. That's when I found "Hope", literally.

I researched counselors in the area, but, because I couldn't work, I didn't have any money to pay. That's when God led me to Hope Family Ministries. Because of amazing people who donate, despite not having any money to pay, I could get the help I needed. When I first came, I was pretty scared and embarrassed. I didn't want to be judged. I didn't want others to think I was weak for not being able to survive. I didn't know if I could fully express everything I was going through to a complete stranger. Not one time did I ever feel judged or looked down upon. I was never made to feel stupid for anything I said. I could talk freely. I could release everything I was bottling up. The weight of my grief was suffocating me, but being able to talk about it helped me breathe again. I felt important and loved. I was validated for my feelings and what I was going through, reassured that I would survive this. I found out that grief is a life-long process. It's not a list I can check off daily or even monthly. It's unpredictable and crazy, but I try to embrace it. I have so many good days now that the few bad days I do have, don't even compare to the beginning of this journey. That's exactly what this is, a journey, my journey. I'm not sure why I was chosen for it, and I don't know what our future holds. God laid this path before me, and I will follow His lead. The future is exciting now. My children and I come to Hope as a family now. We're healing together. Counseling is helping us grow closer. We're not as sad now, and the children are growing through the grief just like I am. We are survivors.

I'll never fully understand why Tyler made the choice that he did. That's what it was, his choice. I choose happiness. I choose joy. I choose not to let grief overtake my life. Even though I can't check my process and journey off on a list, I choose Hope.

Lisa's Story

I enjoy working in a nursing home. I could have worked in many other settings, but a nursing home is where I feel a sense of belonging. The patients become part of our everyday lives because we work where they live. I have laughed and cried with many older souls. The downside to working there is that we see them at the end of their lives and are constantly reminded of our own mortality. I try to be upbeat, because, with their life transitions, they need it.

If you were to ask my co-workers who I am, they would say, "that crazy girl in the therapy department". I have been known to do balloon animals and yo-yo tricks to get smiles. Many times I have heard, "living with you must be so much fun; you're a riot". If my friends only knew! I'm much better now, but for many years I tried to fill the emptiness in my heart with destructive things.

I am a follower of Jesus Christ, a wife and mother, and a witness for how God can change a life. I am married to a minister, living on a farm in Mississippi, but that is definitely not where I started.

My first home was a thousand miles away from Mississippi, a small town in Northwestern Pennsylvania. I had an enjoyable childhood for the most part. In those days, all the kids in our neighborhood played together all day. I was athletic and competitive, so I was often chosen first for teams, which I loved. My parents divorced when I was only three. Mom and I moved in with her mother, Grammy, for a while. Mom remarried and I didn't appreciate my step-dad for a long time.

He wasn't my dad, and I didn't like him because of that. Dad remarried also. My step-mom had no children, and she was not very kind to me.

At the age of nine, an older teenage boy from my neighborhood, showed me pornography and forced me to commit lewd acts with him. When I refused, he'd lock me in a closet until I agreed to them. I'd pray to God. He'd yell at me that there was no God. This traumatized me and caused me to have severe anxiety and flashbacks for many years.

After my paternal grandmother died, I developed severe anxiety about death and funerals, anything related to either. I could have an anxiety attack just driving by a funeral home. I also developed other anxieties about many more things. I had so many fears, I would read, just hide myself away, and create a world of my own in my mind to soothe myself.

From a young age, I've had flashbacks, manic episodes, and severe depressive episodes. I was diagnosed with Bipolar Disorder and prescribed several different medications. I would take them for a while, get better, and stop taking them. I would not take medications when I changed jobs, and couldn't be monitored by my doctor.

I've been in a psychiatric hospital a few times. Once, I signed myself in because my mind was running away like a runaway train. I could tell I was about to crash.

Before salvation, I found solace in illicit relationships, drugs, and alcohol. I struggled with a pornography addiction also. One new job and new coworkers who became friends led to church attendance. I began to learn about God and Christianity. I began to become part of a church family that loved me and that I loved, but I fell into another illicit relationship with a leader in the church.

After salvation, I fell in love with a minister, of all things. I moved to where he lived. He loved me and helped make everything better. I had a flashback one night and almost killed him. My anxiety, depression, and mania, along with my pornography addiction, interfered with our marriage and his ministry also. I had so much trouble attending funerals or visitations with him. I couldn't even attend church, at times, and felt judgment from the congregation constantly.

I was referred to Hope Family Ministries. Bro. Mike was unlike any counselor I'd ever had. He put his hand on his Bible and said, "Either God is telling the truth, or He's a liar. Which is it?" I gave him the answer I knew he wanted, but I didn't believe it. I told him that God is telling the truth. After many weekly counseling sessions, along with long emails to and from Bro. Mike and a couple other friends who pointed me in the right direction, I learned to trust God with my day to day life. I learned to base my decisions on the Word of God rather than on my feelings. I learned to confront lies with truth.

I learned that God had been with me as a child. He'd been with me my entire life. The difference was that I now knew it. God was also in the dark places of my mind, but it wasn't dark any more. I had flashbacks for fifteen years, but, when God became the light in my life taking the darkness away, those didn't control me anymore. I haven't had one in several years. All glory be to God for that!

One thing that I struggled with a lot was forgiveness. How could I forgive my abusers? It would be like saying it was okay for that to happen. It isn't like that at all. What happened to me was wrong, and the people that hurt me were wrong. There is no question about that. What happens to them is not up to me. God has the final say in that. Every moment I spend without forgiveness is a moment lost. "For if you will forgive men their trespasses, your heavenly Father will also forgive you." (Matthew 6:14) If God can forgive, and Jesus lives in me, then I have the strength of Jesus to forgive.

Mike often told me that my feelings, questions, and actions were normal, necessary, and genuine as I worked through this process. Knowing that brought me comfort. Everyone wants to feel "normal". I think everyone is conformed by the world and by their experiences. People do what they have to do to survive. It was understandable that I learned to self-medicate and fantasize. I could put myself anywhere I wanted to in my mind. I could control the situation there better than I could in reality. I have learned to live in the moment. To enjoy the moment. It is tempting to go back there, but the children of Israel wanted to go back to Egypt also. The place that God had for them, the Promised Land, was better than where they wanted to go back to. They just didn't know it at the time.

Mike taught me to fight my fears with scripture. He showed me how to live by the Spirit instead of the flesh. Those two had been in conflict with each other within me. He taught me that, as scripture says, God can meet all my needs. We didn't discuss my fear of death much, it seemed to just work itself out. I take every thought captive. When I think, "I don't want to die." I take it captive and make it obedient to the Word of God. I finish it by saying – "because of Christ, I don't have to". "To be absent from the body is to be present with the Lord." (2 Corinthians 5:8)

I took John 3:16 to be true, and it changed my life. I not only attended a bible study; I led one. I'm no longer afraid to die, for I have life in Christ. I didn't want people to know my past, so I was hiding. Now I openly share my story with people. I'm a healthier wife and mother because of the journey. The blood of Christ not only changes your eternity, it changes your life. All glory be to God!

Freedom

I went from a question mark to an exclamation point because God gave me freedom! What does freedom look like in my life?

Freedom through Jesus has broken down strongholds in my life. I've had the ability to form healthy relationships in love. I see the love of Christ through them.

I'm able to give care to my patients at the end of their lives without fear. I'm able to give them comfort.

I'm able to go to sleep with less fear. I've gone six years without a panic attack or flashback.

I'm a healthier wife, mother and friend because of freedom.

I realize it isn't what I do. It's what Jesus has already done. That takes a load of pressure off because we all mess up.

I'm able to live my life as a child of God, a follower of Jesus. I'm not living my life as a Bipolar, self-medicating, fearful person.

Matt Wilburn, CEO

I never anticipated taking over as CEO for Mike after he retired. That was never even thought of or implied, but it is neat the way things have worked out.

It's been a surprise to me.

After I finished college, I began to feel that I was possibly being called into ministry. I'd been around people who were involved in ministry, and I wouldn't have wished that on my worst enemy. It's not always the most lucrative career. I had a business degree. I planned to make money and retire early with a sailboat. I was discontent working jobs and had no peace. Our pastor at Calvary Baptist Church at that time, Dr. Barnes, really helped me walk through what I was dealing with during that season. God's Spirit, conviction, was working on me. He told me he thought I was being called into ministry. I wanted to tell him he was wrong, but I knew he was right. His next advice to me was to find somewhere to serve while I attended seminary. He thought I needed to work while I was in school. I worked at Bellevue while I was in Mid America Seminary.

I worked part time and then full time while getting a master's degree.

In seminary, I didn't know what I was going to do after I graduated. The president of the seminary did an introductory class. Everybody told what they were called to do. Because I was a "W" and at the back of the class, I had to listen as all my classmates shared their future plans. When it came my turn, I said that I had no idea. I only knew I was supposed to be there that day. The president said he knew exactly how I felt. He said that he felt the same way during his seminary years. That helped me so much because I didn't feel alone in my position. At that time, counseling wasn't offered as a degree. I began to prepare for a career as a pastor or missionary. I learned a lot of Bible. I learned to use the scripture to apply to life's problems. It ended up being great training for what I do now. In Christian Counseling, we need to know how to apply scripture to life. I had to prepare sermons weekly. I was immersed in scripture which was much more applicable to counseling than a degree in the field at that time. I'm grateful that I had the training. I've also been grateful for the business degree which has proved beneficial each day in each job I've held.

I worked part time at Bellevue, then full time as an activities director. It was a great job. It put me around great people. I was able to experience church on a massive scale. It was my job to schedule 1500 kids playing a sport all at the same time. It was a really good administrative experience for me. I was able to observe the workings of all the interoffice relationships and departments. I took a lot away from organizing at those numbers. It was neat for me to be able to be around the pro's, with so many families, so many people there. I had to work with the grounds crew and the administration office about the money. I had to work with all kinds of people and scheduling. I learned a lot. It was a very large church of 30,000. Organizing events for that many people was no small task.

I then pastored a church in Booneville, Calvary Baptist, on a much smaller scale, but I had more jobs. Pastoring a small church of 85-90 involves having about ten jobs at once. I was pastor and yardman. I ran meetings and took care of all the administrative duties. I learned a lot there too that prepared me for my position at Hope later.

When I think back about Hope and its beginnings, I think about watching Mike. We moved here in anticipation of another job. Mike had a job opportunity that fell through. I know that had to be frustrating. I watched him go from a tool and die maker to seminary student. He was only a few years out from his own conversion. He worked a full time job while enrolled in seminary. When his job fizzled out here, he had to go back to tool and die work. I could see where it would feel like those years out in Texas were a waste. All along, we were watching Hope just be born, God's way. When he was first out of seminary, he thought evangelism was his calling. He pursued that for a short time. He was a natural, gifted counselor, though, and didn't even realize he was doing it all along. More and more people wanted to talk with him and spend time being encouraged by conversations they would have with him. I think so many people expect to go into ministry bringing a certain skill set, and expecting to do a certain job. We can't always know how God is going to use us. We don't necessarily know what we're going to do; God can change the script. Throughout it all, Mike stayed faithful to the Lord. His counseling ministry actually began in the machine shop where people would come by to talk to him at his tool box, the most unlikely of places.

I remember coming into our house and having to be quiet because Mike was talking to someone, counseling with someone. I don't think he envisioned this ministry even while he was doing it during the evenings. His church, Calvary Tupelo, supported him in a lot of ways; they were what he needed in the moment. The people around him could see what God was doing through him; they thought it made perfect sense. It's amazing how it all is now just set up, taking place. I'm encouraged when Mike says, "God's going to continue to work". He truly understands that. I remember that all we paid for in the first year here was a trash can. Everything else was paid for. It seems kind of unfair to me to benefit from all his hard work and struggle. I didn't have to go through all the things he went through. When he started the ministry, biblical counseling was thought best left to the professionals.

His credentials were questioned at times, so professionalism was always exhibited. He built the reputation of Hope. He did the work. It is beyond amazing to have a biblically based, donation based, counseling ministry run for twenty-four years. There are less than five in the country. There are a few on the west coast, a few on the east coast, and one in Florida that have been going for more than ten years. I don't think any of those are completely separate from a church or other organization.

When Mike, with the board's backing, approached me about the job of CEO, we discussed how to keep the benefits of his long years of good work from ending up in a file cabinet of wonderful gems, or walking out the door while we started all over again. We are working hard to continue to use what has worked before and build on top of it. One concern we had was "Founders Syndrome". We didn't want Mike to leave and have the ministry die because it was too tied to his name. Obviously, that didn't happen because we have more clients than we can see. They still call wanting to talk to Mike, but they agree to see other counselors. That's evidence of stability for long term. We survived his retirement.

There were times through the early years, when he felt it was over and he was going to have to fold up because there was no money. Mike depended on the faithfulness of the Lord. It was fun to watch. Anyone who comes into Hope benefits from all Mike's hard work. I want to give him all the credit because he deserves it. He was always learning, always growing. Most people didn't see the hard hours, late nights, or two jobs. We saw the good, the bad, and even the ugly. Mike saw it, kept going, and trusting God.

Hope's journey is as much a personal story of Mike's spiritual growth as it is the story of an organization's growth. Because it was tied to him so long, it could only do as well as he did. That's a testament to him. If Hope does well, it's clear that Mike did well. He could choose to go fishing now, but he still has a heart for ministry. He's been an absolute gem through the transition. The things that have been easy for me are easy because he made them easy. He made everything as easy as possible. Well, he made it all possible. Hope's long term goal, our end game, is to still be here fifty years from now, offering the same donation-based, quality service. The counseling is here. Our counselors are all booked. I just want that to continue.

Actual Notes from Former Clients

...One of the most unique ministries in the country; true biblical counseling with an emphasis on the soul.

...Jesus Christ continues to set the captives free...

Thanks for the encouragement and the relentless challenge. I will never be the same

The Lord has used you in such a mighty way in our lives.

God has touched the lives of generations of family members through your obedience to Him.

Thank you for your commitment to helping individuals and families find God's will for their lives.

We are so grateful for your work.

Your ministry has been a blessing to me and many others.

Lives have been changed because of your obedience to the Lord.

I can think of nothing that we need more than the Hope that only Jesus Christ can bring.

Thank you for just talking to me about my dad and about my mom, what I worry about. You changed my life. (Written in crayon)

I am so grateful for your words of kindness and hope.

When I first came to Hope Family Ministries, I was a very angry woman.

Week by week, God began to reveal to me that it was not my job to change or control my husband. It was, however, my responsibility to seek Him with my whole heart and allow Him to change ME whether or not my husband or situation ever changed.

I wanted to share how blessed our lives are because we renewed our commitment to each other, and to our Lord.

I didn't have much hope for my life and relationships to improve, but your ministry has restored my perspective. I can live every day counting my blessings and cherishing every moment with people in my life who love me!

You helped me so much with my faith and perspective, and I relied daily on the things you taught me. The verse that meant the most to me was
Isaiah 30:21. I wasn't even very familiar with it until now – it's my "go to" verse!

As one who has been helped so much through your ministry, I know what a great work of God it is!

I'm learning more every day how to trust and believe, and how to get back up after I fall down.

Thank you for your words of wisdom. When I left your office last, I pulled into a parking lot and called my dad... We didn't talk long because he was so weak, but the time was very precious to me. The release of pent-up emotions – well I simply don't have words.

I have never felt I was just another client to see, or that it was routine during our session. I am sure others have experienced the same. I believe you have prayed beforehand, and, then, seek wisdom as we talk.

I am grateful that Hope Family Ministries is rooted and founded upon the Word of God and prayer.

Thank you for praying for me. God healed me; my pain is gone out of my body. I can continue doing the ministry for the tribal children. I know that God has a purpose and plan for my whole life.

Thank you for all you do for people in need like me. Thank you for being there at my lowest point in life.

I thank God for His anointed network in you, crossing denominational lines in building relationships that e POWER and PURITY.

Our daughter was in a very rebellious time in her life, and we were struggling with how to handle the situation. Your counsel confirmed what I felt in my heart, but was too confused and scared to sort in my mind. Listen, model faith, grace, Fruit of the Spirit, don't define repentance in her life, of her questioning – our love should never be questioned, celebrate every time she comes home, home should be a place of love and acceptance, her obedience to us should not be the test of fellowship-remember the Pharisees, don't measure her by the bad choices she makes, believe in her, don't alienate her "till she gets it right", stay involved.

Your counsel strengthened me when I was at a breaking point. It also freed me to not only love her unconditionally, but also to express that love.

Bro. Mike Marecle

HOPEFAMILYMINISTRIES.COM

(662) 842-4673

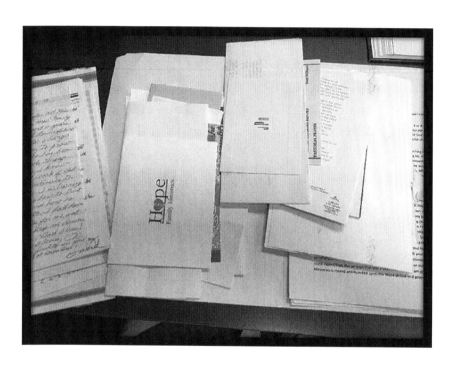

Made in the
USA
Columbia, SC